EDGAR KALLANDS

Kaltag

EDGAR KALLANDS

Kaltag

P.O. Box 1214 Fairbanks, Alaska 99707

ISBN 0-910871-00-0

Copyright 1982 Yukon-Koyukuk School District of Alaska

Produced By: Yukon-Koyukuk School District of Alaska
Superintendent: Joe Cooper
Assistant-superintendent: Fred Lau
Project Coordinator: Don Kratzer
Interviewing and Editing: Curt Madison and Yvonne Yarber
Photography: Curt Madison [unless otherwise noted]

Material collected during September 1979 in Kaltag, Alaska.

Project funded by the following sources:
   Johnson O'Malley Grant – E00C14202164
   Indian Education Grant – 84.060

Regional School Board:
Donald Honea Sr. - Chairman
Fred Lee Bifelt - Vice Chairman
Eddie Bergman
Dixie Dayo - Clerk
Pat McCarty

Library of Congress
Cataloging in Publication Data
Madison, Curt
Yarber, Yvonne
  Edgar Kallands - Kaltag. A Biography
  YKSD Biography Series
  ISBN 0-910871-00-0
  1. Kallands, Edgar 2. Koyukon Athabaskan-
Alaska Biography

SPIRIT MOUNTAIN PRESS
P.O. Box 1214 Fairbanks, Alaska 99707

Title Page - Edgar Kallands as a boy, with his father hauling wood in Tanana.
Oregon Province Jesuit Archives, Gonzaga University

A Note From a Linguist

As you read through this autobiography you will notice a style and a diction you may not have seen before in print. This is because it is an oral storytelling style. This autobiography has been compiled from many hours of taped interviews. As you read you should listen for the sound of the spoken voice. While it has not been possible to show all the rhythms and nuances of the speaker's voice, much of the original style has been kept. If possible you should read aloud and use your knowledge of the way the old people speak to recapture the style of the original.

This autobiography has been written in the original style for three reasons. First, the original style is a kind of dramatic poetry that depends on pacing, succinctness, and semantic indirectness for its narrative impact. The original diction is part and parcel of its message and the editors have kept that diction out of a deep respect for the person represented in this autobiography.

The second reason for keeping the original diction is that it gives a good example of some of the varied richness of the English language. English as it is spoken in many parts of the world and by many different people varies in style and the editors feel that it is important for you as a reader to know, understand and respect the wide resources of this variation in English.

The third reason for writing in the original style is that this style will be familiar to many of you who will read this book. The editors hope that you will enjoy reading something in a style that you may never have seen written before even though you have heard it spoken many times.

Ron Scollon
Alaska Native Language Center
University of Alaska
Fairbanks
1979

Acknowledgements

Many people have helped make this book possible. Edgar's wife, Virginia gave her comments. Hazel, Glenn, Arlo, and Tassie Olsen gave their house. Ron Scollon gave an insight into language. Bea Hagen typed the transcripts while Cheryl DeHart did the final manuscript. Despite all advances in age Bob Maguire continues to be the original instigator although he's an outside one now. Fred Lau and Joe Cooper provide administrative support and Mavis Brown does endless work. The Manley Hot Springs Community School Committee provides the work space in the old Manley School. And the Yukon-Koyukuk School District Regional Board continue to pay the bills. Janis Carney and Cheryl DeHart donated proofreading time.

The extensive use of archive photographs would not be possible without the guidance of Renee Blahuta, University of Alaska Archivist.

Thank you.

Foreword

Edgar Kallands-Kaltag is the tenth in a series of autobiographies of people who live in the eleven villages serviced by the Yukon-Koyukuk School District. These books are designed for students living in rural Alaska although they may well captivate readers of any age.

The series is meant to fill the void created by school materials that all come from Outside and carry that bias. Alaska need not be described as a "barren wasteland" on the periphery of the real world. This is the center of a rich and varied and, unfortunately, neglected culture. We hope to bring home some relevance of curriculum through this series.

Edgar Kallands, and many other of the people in this series, is familiar to the students of the middle Yukon River. This story offers students the opportunity to take a look closer to home and to study some of the changes that have taken place in a historically short period of time.

The story of Edgar Kallands is written in four chapters. This offers teachers easy breaking points for discussion and activities. The book is by no means a definitive work. It should be viewed as a beginning point for teachers in classrooms throughout the Interior.

Edgar Kallands has been written in the diction and style of the story teller. As his speech is that of many students, it may allow easy reading. For others it is an introduction to the richness of the English language. Enjoy.

Curt Madison
Yvonne Yarber
April 22, 1981
Manley Hot Springs, Alaska

The Steamer Sarah *on the last day of September, 1913.* Harry M. Devane Collection, University of Alaska Archives

Table of Contents

Note from a Linguist	5
Acknowledgements	6
Foreword	7
Maps	10
Introduction	11

CHAPTER ONE — GROWING UP

Kallands	12
Tanana School	16
Learned from Dad	19
Having a Good Time	23

CHAPTER TWO — STEAMBOATS AND DIESEL POWER

Deckhand and Fireman	26
Promises	30
Boats All Over the River	33

CHAPTER THREE — WINTER WORK WITH DOGS

Mail Carrier	41
Serum Run	43
Trapping	49

CHAPTER FOUR — KALTAG TODAY

Store and Post Office	54
School Board	58
Changes	59

INDEX	63

Local Area

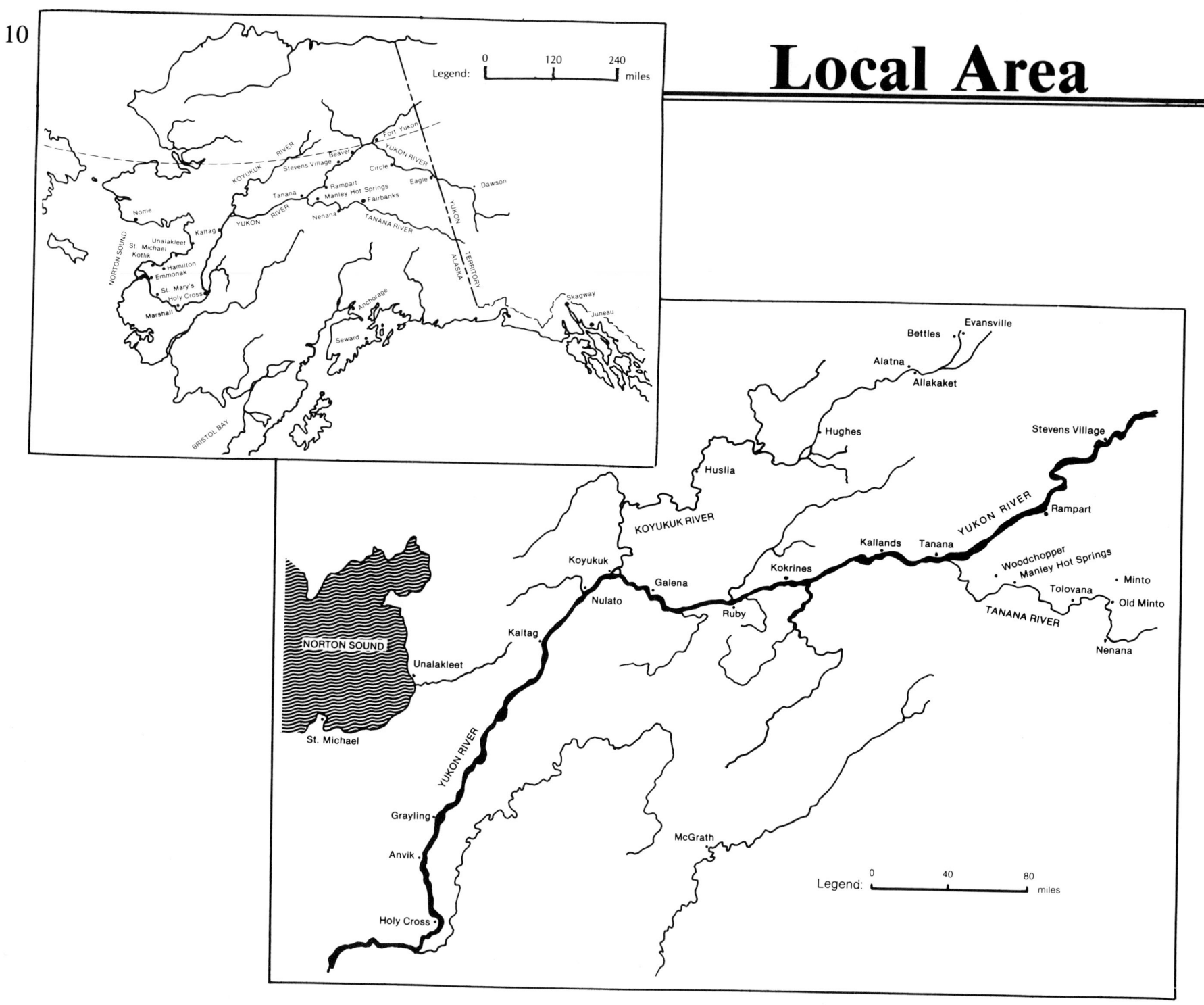

Introduction

Edgar Kallands lives in Kaltag, an Athabaskan village on the Yukon River end of a traditional trade route to Unalakleet on the Norton Sound coast. There are about 240 people in Kaltag, a school, church, four stores, community center, and town council building. It is an active town constantly mixing the old ways with new developments.

Although Edgar is best known for his part in the famous Serum Run to Nome popularized by the Iditarod Sled Dog Race, it cannot match his years as an expert riverboat engineer and captain.

Edgar Kallands died late 1981. He was unable to see his book in print. But he was able to go over the final manuscript in April 1981 at the Alaska Native Medical Center in Anchorage. Virginia was always close at hand. She generously helped with final details for this book when Edgar appeared to need rest from the stress of recounting a lifetime of joys and sadness.

As you read this book you may recall other stories you have heard about Edgar.

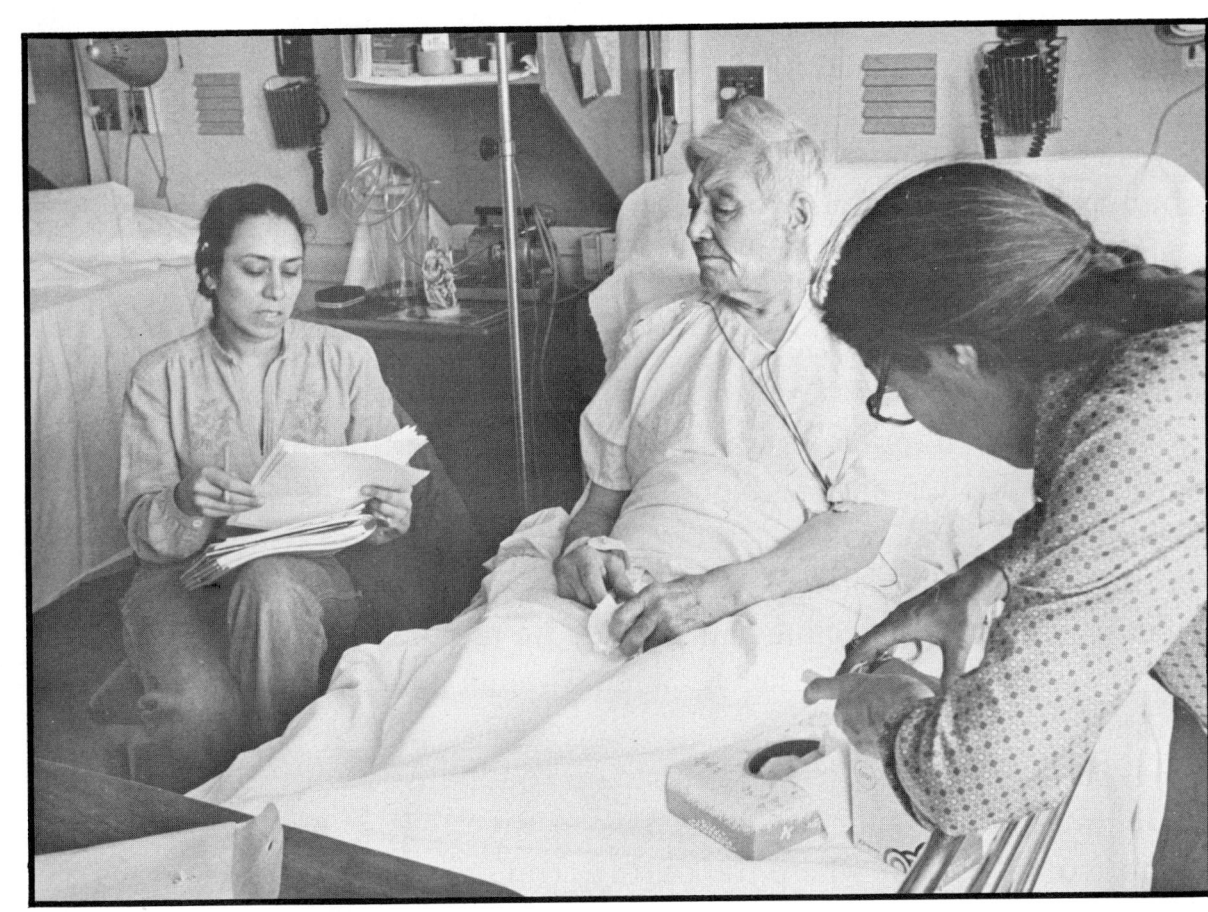

Yvonne Yarber reading the manuscript to Edgar in the ANS hospital in Anchorage. Edgar's daughter Anna listens in. April 1981.

Chapter One: Growing Up

Kallands

My father's name was Alexander Kallands, better known as Harry Kallands. Born and raised in Trinity Bay, St. John's, Newfoundland. The way he told it, it was a big family. His mother had died and his father remarried. I guess he didn't get along with his stepmother or something. So he ran away from home when he was age fifteen. I don't know. He just wanted to get away I guess.

He went out and grandbanked. You know what grandbanking is? It's fishing for tomcod in the open rowboats off the banks of Newfoundland. He did that for three years and ended up down along the East Coast and joined the Navy. He was in that for about three years until he got typhoid fever.

The gold strike in Alaska was on about the time he got cured. So he hopped on board a three-masted schooner coming around from Boston into Nome. When he got off the ship in Nome he had one dollar. But somehow he ended up coming up into the Yukon River and appeared in Nulato. That's where he met my mother, Angeline Titi. When he met her he was carrying mail for Corbusier between Tanana and Nulato once a month.

1903 they got married and started a roadhouse about thirty-five miles below Tanana on the Yukon River. It's an overnight stop from Tanana, where the portage trail goes across and comes out at the mouth of Mason Creek Slough. The trail makes a big shortcut rather than following the river.

Edgar Kallands in Tanana at seven.
Oregon Province Jesuit Archives, Gonzaga University

Dad said a survey team was there and done surveying one summer. That was their base camp. I guess they named the place Kallands after my dad because he had a roadhouse there.

I was born in Kallands, October 18, 1904. I have my baptism certificate signed by Father Ragaru, one of the first Jesuits in this country. They gave me the names of Edward, Edgar and Edmond. Father Ragaru told my dad, "I got to give him a name too." So he named me one of those. I don't know which one it was.

I was young when we stayed in Kallands so I don't remember everything. All I know is eat in the morning. Get up in the morning. I don't know what time. I hated to go to bed but I had to. And when I got up in the morning my mother said, "You got to write your ABC's and numbers up to one hundred." That was it. So before we ever got moved away and went to Tanana I knew all that.

I know we used to have a great time as kids. There was about four or five houses at Kallands. There was John Minook and his family. Little Paul and his family. Mr. and Mrs. Langford and their daughter, our family and Little Henry's family. Little Henry had four or five boys and three or four girls right next door to us. Just a hop, skip and a jump from house to house.

I remember the roadhouse and seeing people coming through. It was about twenty-six feet long by about eighteen feet wide with eight bunks in there. Our house was built on to it. Everybody ate in the kitchen off to one side of the house. And they had a garden, I know that.

I watched Dad cut wood for steamboats there at Kallands. You didn't have to have a contract then. Long as you had a woodpile on the bank, steamboats would buy wood. At that time there was about twenty-five steamboats up and down the river. Twenty-five different ones! Well, you see, all the freight come in from St. Michael, up the river.

There was the Steamer *Sarah, Susie-Louise,* the *St. Michael* and *Minneapolis, Julia B., Delta,* the *Reliance* with Captain George Green, and Jack Green was on the Steamer *Alaska* later on. And there was the Steamer *Alice* and *Tanana.* The *William Isem* was one of the biggest at that time on the river. It went from San Francisco to Alaska and paid for herself that one trip. It ran on the Yukon after that. Then there was the two Army transports, the Steamer *General J. W. Jacobs* and *Jeff Davis.* Then down from Dawson there was the *Whitehorse* and the *Kaska.* Later on was the Steamer *Yukon,* sister ship to the *Alaska.* So, you see, that all took a lot of wood.

I remember at that time I had only one pet dog. He was my dog, or I was his dog. One or the other. No matter what I tried, I couldn't run away from him. He was raised up with me. My dad had a team of dogs. They obeyed him real well, but they were crazy dogs. They didn't do nothing but go. That's right. Three and a half hours from Kallands to Tanana. Around thirty-five miles with Mother and I on the sled. Of course, the trail those days was just as hard as a floor.

There was three mail teams on the route between Tanana and Ruby. Two of them was always on the trail. Plus your team and his team and somebody elses. You could start out and walk right from Tanana to Ruby and have beautiful walking. You didn't have to worry about breaking through the trail, it was that hard. You could even start in Fairbanks and walk all the way to Unalakleet and have a place to stop every night.

Then it was hard going from Unalakleet all the way towards Nome.

I can remember a time we started out from Kallands and had a brand new sled. Dad, mamma and me going to Kokrines. And as I was saying, those were crazy dogs. Well, we didn't even get four miles out of Kallands before the dogs seen a squirrel or something and away they went. Dad couldn't stop them in time. When we did stop, why the sled was broke back to the second stanchion. He turned the dogs around and went back home. Got another sled from Little Henry and went on to Kokrines anyhow.

We lived in Kallands till I was about seven years old. Then we moved to Tanana so I could go to school. I had to learn my ABC's a little better.

Tanana Public School class of 1912. Edgar is in the back row, second from right.
Ben Mozee Collection, University of Alaska Archives

Tanana School

I went by the name Edward up to the time I moved to Tanana. But there was two of us in school named Edward. Everytime the teacher called "Edward;" we'd both raise our hand. That's when I decided to use Edgar instead. That way, we knew which one had to raise our hand.

The first teacher I had was a Native half-breed, Jesse Harper, born in Tanana. She went Outside and got her teaching degrees. Then I had Mr. Mozee, he married Jesse Harper.

I'm going to tell you one thing what used to happen in Tanana when I was going to school. Well, the first boat down river after breakup was coming into Tanana. As soon as the whistle blew, regardless of what time it was, school was out. Just like that. We all went up with the teacher to see the boat land, and people come and go. After about half an hour we'd all go back to school again. That was it for the first boat. After that, no matter how many boats come in, we were still in school.

At that time it was very quiet in school. You dropped a pencil and it was just like dropping a log. Boy, you could hear it all over the room. We had no disturbance in school. Everything was real quiet. It was a public school. Looking back on it now, we learned more when we were in fourth grade than these children learn now in high school.

We knew all our times tables backwards and forwards. It didn't matter which time tables the teacher pulled on you, it's just automatic for us. And we knew our geography from A to Z as the saying goes. We knew all our States and capitals and

Edgar with the soldiers at Fort Gibbon in Tanana. "I used to sneak in to get my picture taken with the soldiers."
Edgar Kallands Collection

all the principal cities and the manufacturing items they were making. You ask these high school kids now and they don't know. I was surprised. Like, I asked my grandchildren how they were making out on their times tables. They didn't know their times tables. I went after them right away. I says, "You got to learn that."

When I was in school I really had my mind worked up so that I could remember. For a while I could just read a whole paragraph in a book and practically give it right back out, word for word. I had a wonderful memory but it's just lately beginning to falter, since I had this stroke.

I never missed any days of school. I may have been late a few times, but I was in school all the time. All the students were there steady, year round. They didn't have to go out trapping, in and out of town. When I went to school in

School in Steven's Village around 1920.

Edgar Kallands Collection

Tanana it was practically all White children. There was only about six of us that were Native or part Native. There was Marie Anicich, Margaret Peterson (now Kokrine), and the Kee girls who were Eskimo and Chinese, and myself. One of us that's alive is Anna Pickett, who was Kee. The rest were all White children. White people were living in the town city limits mostly for the Army being there, Fort Gibbon, at Tanana. There was a lot of White help with work or businesses.

Most of the Native people lived at the Mission three miles up river. Their children went to school at the Episcopal Mission there. I didn't go up to the Mission myself, even for the potlatches. The Mission was off limits too for the Army. That's all I know about the Mission. I didn't mingle with the people, you know. I was in the same town with some Natives, but I lost contact with talking the Native language.

You see, my mother was Native. She was born somewhere around the vicinity of Kaltag or Nulato. Nobody seems to know. And she died before I had a chance to find out. When she was alive I was around Native people and she would speak Native with me. But I lost her when I was only nine.

Mother had dropsey far as I know. That's all my father told me, the doctors couldn't do anything for her. So after she died I just lost the language until 1923 when my father died. That's when I start to go with Native people. I've been mingling with Natives ever since.

Edgar's mother Angeline. Taken about 1911.
Oregon Province Jesuit Archives, Gonzaga University

Learned from Dad

After Mother died, my father was the only person teaching me. Of course, I still went to school. And Dad wanted me to take special arithmetic instruction with Father Jetté after school. So I did. Two hours every night. He was very pleasant and instructive. He wasn't overbearing. He'd break everything down and explain it so nice to you. He was right with the children. The kids all liked him. And in church when he read the missal, or anything, you understood every word, no matter what grade you were in. He cut everything down so you could understand it. Very learned.

He gave me my first 3-A camera. It's the old Kodak post card size. Father Jetté used that one first, then he used a different style, a box-type Graflex. He done all his developing and printing himself. I learned how to develop and print with him. We must have had about eighty dollars worth of different kinds of papers to develop and print with. Four different kinds of paper, Velox brand. I took a lot of pictures.

Like I was saying, I learned quite a little from Dad. I learned how to do a little farming. I used to hate to weed the garden. We had about an acre. But the biggest part of that acre was oat-hay for the horse, so that was easy. The rest was turnips, carrots, radish, rutabagas and enough potatoes for ourselves. Then he had a little flower garden too.

Tanana, when I was growing up, everybody had a garden. I don't care where you went, where you looked. Everybody's

"That's the Kodak folding camera Father Jette gave me. I took a lot of pictures in this book with it." Edgar Kallands Collection

Loading up the wagon in Holy Cross. Edgar Kallands Collection

front yard had a garden. They always had pride in their gardens. When fall came and everything came out of the ground, oh gee, that was when it tasted good.

There was quite a few horses in Tanana at that time. Arthur J. Cambell had four teams, Cris Able one team, and Joe Anicich had one horse. The NC Company had a little horse they used for delivery from the store. The Army had both horses and mules. I don't know how many teams.

Dad had an old horse then. Poor fellow. He hauled in the dray business. Dad used him to haul stuff from the steamboat landing to the different places in town. He delivered water around town up until '22. Then he bought a horse by the name of Pepper. A rightful name for the boy. He was just full of pepper but a heck of a nice horse. Full of life is all. He was my pet. Period.

All the people that had horses had barns for them, plenty oat-hay and hay. The horse was your locomotion so you had a nice warm barn with a stove for him. The only time he was cold was when he was out standing still. Otherwise, when he got in the barn he was nice and warm all the time. Least that's the way I've seen them at Tanana. Nice and warm.

The most important thing I learned from Dad was survival. He took me out one year, the last year he was alive. I was 17 years old. Just promoted to the sixth grade when I went out. You see I was late getting to school. I was moving along alright as far as I was concerned. Anyway, we built a house up Dall River.

Went up there the hard way. We rowed and poled the boat. Had to make two trips. Go ahead one day. Come back. Go back the next day and then take the load on to the next camp site. We went up the whole river and finally got to where the water was too shallow to have much easy going. We stopped and made camp and built a house there.

We whip-sawed some lumber for next spring. Never used it. Dad died in the meantime. Died in March. I knew he was sick. I wanted to take him to Fairbanks. Wanted to go across the Brooks Trail to Fairbanks from Stevens Village but he wouldn't go.

He died the 26th of March, 1923, 7:30 in the evening in Opie Russell's store at Stevens Village. As far as I can read on all the symptons, he had pleurisy which turned into pneumonia. There was no doctor. We had no medicine for him. So he died exactly nine years and nine days and five hours difference from Mother. I know they sent for me in school about three o'clock when Mother died in Tanana.

We buried him about three days later. Opie Russell made a coffin out of one big redwood board. I stayed with Russell for

Hauling wood in Tanana. Edgar Kallands as a boy and his father. Oregon Province Jesuit Archives, Gonzaga University

maybe two weeks. He treated me real well. But I felt like I was encroaching so I got out again. I know one time I wanted some sweets so I say, "How much is cookies?" He told me, so I went out and weighed up a pound and paid him.

He told me, "You don't have to buy anything as long as you're with me here." But I didn't look at it that way. I was never brought up that way. It was either my own or it wasn't. That's the way I felt. Because my dad was really independent the same way.

I had nothing against my dad. Whatever I wanted, I always asked and I'd get the money from him. And when I made any money I'd just give it to my dad. I'd never think about anything at all. He didn't drink it up so I didn't have to worry there. My dad was a very, very moderate drinker. He'd take a drink once in a while. All during prohibition he had his own whiskey. Never bothered.

I seen him happy one night. When prohibition went into effect, 1918. He came home with whole bunch of bottles. He said, "I got to go back and get some more." I was asleep when he come back. Next thing I know, next morning. Eight o'clock there's breakfast. That's all there was to it.

One time too he come home late. March I guess, 1921 or '22. It's the first time I ever see my dad really out. He come in, he says, "Ed, put the horse away. I can't take care of him." Cold outside so I put on my coat, went out, brought a couple buckets of water in the house. I took the horse into the barn. Took his harness off. I wiped him all down. Dried him off as best I could and throw a blanket over him. Nice warm barn anyhow. I had the fire going in there. Get a little dry timothy hay in there and I went back into the house. Dad was sound asleep.

Then about six o'clock that night I went out and fed the horse some oats and hay. Give him some water. About half past nine I went out again and cleaned his stall. Threw some old hay underneath him, fed him, put some water in his manger. I checked the fire, went home and went to bed. Next thing I know, breakfast. Dad had it ready. Never missed breakfast every morning. He cooked for me. He raised me.

I never got a licking from my dad. A lot of talking but never a licking. I was happy. I sure missed him. I think I learned quite a little from Dad. Probably more so than if I'd went somewhere else for school. He wanted to know if I wanted to go to BIA school in Chemawa, Oregon or to Mission school in Holy Cross. I balked on both of them. Told him, "I want to be with you."

Having a Good Time

Spring after my father died I stayed in Stevens with Essau Roberts. There was only about fifteen houses there at Stevens and we used to go up to the Mission. All of us young folk just walk up there. That's when I start to be with Native people again. One middle-aged lady up there, Belle Stevens, started me in to talking Native language. Because the other young people, they started in to talk to me too. But they were having lots of fun when they were talking to me. They tell me certain kinds of words and they weren't giving me the right answer either. It'd be something else. So this Belle Stevens, she taught me words right. I began to pick it up from there.

It was more fun growing up at Tanana you know. I was

Edgar walking across the top of the Nenana railroad bridge. Edgar Kallands Collection

only eighteen and there was a whole young crowd at that time. We were all running around together and having a good time. I went out hunting with the men, young fellows. That time there was no drinking either. Not like now, goodness sakes. These kids here is drinking at eight, nine, ten years old. I don't know what's going to happen. I really don't.

Then the summer after my dad died I was all alone, so I was more freer. I still lived my own life, my own way. That's the only way I knew anyhow. But I was a loner. I lived by myself there in Tanana at my Dad's house. For a while I'd go down to the pool room and play pool.

One Sunday in 1925 playing ball against Nenana. Edgar played second base and took the picture.
Edgar Kallands Collection

Rat hunting in the flats. We just came into camp and Esau Roberts jumped into his tent when I took the picture. Edgar Kallands Collection

    Then that winter for a while bunch of us boys and girls used to congregate in one house, like Lee's or Kee's, even the Lockwoods. Their mother and father would be there. We'd play game of Five Hundred, six no-trump. Sometimes we'd play Rummy. We'd have a great time playing cards like that until ten o'clock at night. Then we'd all head our different directions to go home. We'd all be over at another house tomorrow night. Just having a good time.

    I had to think about making a living so I went hunting rats that spring after I lost my dad. Went with a fellow name of Benjamin Steven. We got a little over two hundred rats. Then I went to work on the steamboats.

Chapter Two: Steamboats and Diesel Power

Deckhand and Fireman

I remember my dad used to say, "Ed, don't ever work on the boats." But since he died when I was eighteen I had nowhere to turn. I had no relatives in Tanana. So I went to the steamboats. I guess he didn't think I'd ever get anywhere, I'd ever be anything but a deckhand.

After I went out hunting rats that spring I went to work on the Steamer *Alaska*. Decking. Up to Dawson and back again.

Handling freight, wood, all the dirty stuff on the boat. You might say the deckhand's job is taking care of the boat. I saw some new places that year.

The next year I went to work on the Steamer *Yukon*. Went up the same route to Dawson and back. Couple trips. Then I stayed in Tanana and worked as a deckhand on the Steamer *Jacobs*. One day, lo and behold, we got a new second mate, Fred Racey, the mate I worked under on the Steamer *Yukon*. He was real strict and I mean strict. You did what he told you to do or you got a good talking to. But I liked him regardless. I didn't pay any attention to what other people said. I never had any trouble with him. In fact the second year I worked on the Steamer *Jacobs* I was third mate under him. He'd tell me what he wanted done and even though I was still a deckhand I could tell the other men to work. We'd work the same shift. Get through, no trouble. He was a good mate and he knew his business.

Steamer Whitehorse *freighting on the Yukon.*

Elby Davis Collection, University of Alaska Archives

I worked under a couple different mates then I had a chance to move up to being a fireman. They needed a fireman and I wanted to go firing but the Chief Engineer wouldn't hire me because I was under the mate yet. So I went and talked to the mate. There was more money firing and it was easier. As a deckhand you worked six hours on and six hours off. And you might work twenty-four hours straight unloading freight. Firing you were on six hours and off twelve and you got twenty-five dollars a month more.

"Ed," the mate told me, "I don't want to hold you back from making more money. If you can get somebody to take your place, I'll let you go." We were loading a barge there in Nenana, but he let me go uptown. I came back in an hour with another man. So I went firing. Leon M. Dow was Chief Engineer and Walter Johnson was his assistant.

I started out firing coal with a big Swede, or Norwegian, by the name of Axel Johnson. As long as he was in the fire hole there was nothing to worry about. Look at the steam and keep the fire going. Nothing to it. But the first day I was on shift and the boat was leaving, I was all alone. Poor old Axel came back from uptown on a real wingdinger. Staggering around. He laid down counting fairies in bed I guess. I was on shift and I was all alone.

What am I going to do? I've got to hold 200 pounds of steam that's all there is to it. For about twenty minutes it was pretty shakey. But I finally got her stoked right and home free. The main thing about firing you had to keep your fire stoked right and the right amount of water in the boiler. We had two marks to watch on the glass. If the water fell too low, you had to add more water. Just go back and give a little steam to the feed pump so the water could go in the boiler. I got so I could make four trips in six hours and manipulate the valves. It could damage the boiler if the water got too low. And if you got too much water the engine could pull water out into the steam. Instead of getting dry steam into the pistons you'd get wet steam. That'd condense in the cylinder and you'd have a knock. If you got too much water, the piston could blow the head right off.

When you got off shift you had to leave a clean fire for your relief. Make sure the clinkers are out and the grates are clean and the steam is up. We had to hold 220 pounds underway and 175 when we're tied up.

The steamers Schwatka, Yukon *and* Susie, *tied up at Tanana.* Elby Davis Collection, University of Alaska Archives

Promises

I worked seven or eight seasons, forty-five months total, firing and the old man got after me. The Chief, L.M. Dow. I wouldn't listen to him. He wanted me to study books. I promised him but I didn't go through with my promise that winter. "You've got all the practical knowledge, now get the book knowledge," he says. "Read up."

"Okay, Chief, I'll do that," I said. But that's as far as it got. He went after George Adams the same way. We were both nice boys. We both faithfully promised. And we both faithfully broke our promise. We didn't read up on the books at all.

Next spring when I got on the boat and told the Chief I didn't read the books he really let both of us have it. I promised I'd start reading right then. He says, "Who's going to take my place? Who's going to take Walter Johnson's place? You boys have got to do it. We can't last forever."

The inspectors weren't due before August so I had lots of time. We started reading the books anyway. While George was oiling I was reading the book and the other way around on my shift. Then suddenly when we got to Marshall, the inspectors were already there!

I knew the other inspectors. I'd known them all my life, but these were two new guys from Outside. Dickert and another fellow. The old man didn't know them either so he began feeling them out. It took him two days to feel them out while George and I were reading the books like mad. It was nightmare for five days. Oiling, reading the book and

Steamer Julia B. *with her barges tied up in Tanana.*   Thaggard Buchholz Collection, University of Alaska Archives

answering questions. We had over 125 questions and a couple were really ticklish. If you missed one of those two you failed and had to wait another year before you could take the test again. One had to do with bursting power of the boiler plate and the stay bolts that held the plate on. The other was setting the weight a certain distance from the fulcrum of the safety valve. Both George and I passed.

Later the inspector told us, "Ed, George, the trouble with you boys is you were scared of me." He was right. We were really on edge. We didn't know him before. Right from Outside, we had never seen him before. Who was he and how was he going to treat us?

When we got to Tanana I had to go in for a physical examination. The doctor said I had astigmatism in one eye and wrote down incompetent. I didn't think anything of it, but the Chief got really mad. It delayed my license for a year until I could get glasses from an Army doctor in Galena.

The license was for rivers only and up to 1200 horsepower engines. That included the Steamer *Nenana*. I never worked on that boat but I did work on the *Barry K.* and it had a bigger engine yet. It had a sixteen inch cylinder and a seven foot stroke. One of the strongest boats on the river. Right now my license is First Assistant Engineer, 1000 horsepower, any tonnage and Third Assistant Engineer, any tonnage, any waters. I've renewed it seven times and that's what it is today.

Boats All Over the River

When I started there were boats all over the river. Coming and going all the time. Kids run down to the bank, wood cutting camps, long-shoring and cheap travel up and down the river. After the railroads came in, the steamboats work was cut down. Towards the end there were four boats really because the Steamer *Alaska* and Steamer *Yukon* mostly carried tourists. Between Dawson and Nenana they'd have a hundred tourists each way. There was a regular circuit. They'd come into the Interior on the railroad either from Skagway to Dawson or Seward to Nenana and complete the circuit on the sternwheelers. They were mostly elite Whites coming in from Stateside.

They really enjoyed their trip. The steamboat was a traveling hotel, dining room, waiters, three meals a day and midnight lunch. Coming from Dawson the boat would stop at Eagle and maybe stay a couple hours then take off down for Circle or Fort Yukon. Stop just for the tourists to walk around. The boat would blow the half hour whistle, fifteen minute whistle, and the five minute whistle and go. They stopped at Eagle, Circle, Fort Yukon, Beaver, Stevens Village, Rampart, Tanana. Hot Springs was four miles from the river so sometimes they

A tour boat on the slough in Manley Hot Springs about 1920. Charles Bunnell Collection, University of Alaska Archives

didn't stop there. They put off mail and that was it. There was a landing there. Tolovana and Minto they didn't stop and Nenana was the end of the line.

Those of us working on the boat just waited while we were tied up. Sometimes we went ashore to get something from the store but right back to the boat. We were tied up to the boat, but the tourists would walk around, buy Native beadwork and trinkets at the store and take pictures.

Stores had all kinds of trinkets for them. Natives did a lot of sewing, mooseskin, beadwork, parkies. Later when I worked in the store at Tanana, it was nothing when the tourists came to take in five or six hundred dollars in a couple hours.

Steamer Sarah *going past Ruby, July 4, 1917.*   Lula Fairbanks Collection, University of Alaska Archives

They put me in fireman's position at $115 a month. George Adams was getting $3,000 for the summer season. Good money in those days. The way I saw it I deserved as much as George Adams so I quit and went with N.C. Company.

George Adams worked up to getting a Chief Engineer license but it almost killed him. I saw him in the hospital and asked him what happened. He said, "What if something breaks. I keep thinking what if something breaks. How can I stop it?"

I told him, "George, it's metal, it's a machine. Of course it's going to break. You can't stop it. Your job is to fix it and get going after it breaks. You can't worry yourself that way."

I worked two and a half seasons on the *Barry K.* as First Assistant Engineer under Fred Dorn, 1942 - '44. He took his watch six o'clock in the morning, then I'd take it in the afternoon. He came back on from six o'clock in the evening till midnight and I was on again. It was good money for those days too, $3,200 a season. 1945 I worked on the Steamer *Yukon*.

The next year a fellow named Harold Stewart working for the NC Co. asked me to go down to Marshall and spend the summer as a deckhand with him. $1,500 for the season and I got raises the next two years.

The company was Alaska Commercial first, then it was Northern Navigation, NN Co. When they got out of navigation it was NC Co. In 1923 it became NC Co. of Alaska. Pretty soon they dropped the end. It was NC Co. until they quit in 1972. At one time they had twenty-five steamboats on the river and twenty-two stores.

The third year I went right up to the pilot house. 1950 I was skipper of the boat with a crew working under me. The

Mildred was sixty-four feet long, fourteen feet wide and ran on two 75 horsepower diesel Cat engines. We handled freight and mail. It got to where we had four men on deck, a cook and myself.

We built a recreation room on the front of the cabin twelve feet long. It was well insulated so wherever we were we had a nice place. When we tied up in the evening we'd play cards there. We had a table ran the length with storage under it. The cook brought the meals up and we brought the dishes back to the galley to be washed. We had a home on that boat. Period.

The whole crew was hired from Kotlik. The village used to be Chiniliak but it flooded out every fall so they moved to Kotlik. It seemed like the men from St. Michael were drinking too much to be a crew on the boat. I told the boys I'll do all the drinking for the crew all summer. That's the way I'd like to have it and it was. I had no trouble.

Crossing in the ocean from the mouth of the Yukon to St. Michael could be pretty scarey. We only drew three feet with

Steamboats and barges tied up at St. Michael. John Zug Collection, University of Alaska Collection

the boat and the waves could be five or six feet easy. I always said to the crew when we get to St. Michael, "I want everything cleaned up and everything put away on the barge, shipshape. Then you can go. I wouldn't let them take care of the other barges. There was a shipyard crew of six men to keep their own barges clean. I balked at them asking for my crew. They kept our barge clean before going ashore. That way we're ready to go if the wind starts to blow.

If it got windy the boys came right back to the boat, cleaned off the engine and we were off. Lot of times we didn't go ashore either. We just stayed on board and played cards. Edward Andrews and his brother used to have an awful time trying to get me in Crazy Eights and Pick-Two. We had a good time. Nobody was mad at one another. We had a lot of fun. We were just one. And nobody drank. Not even me and I did the drinking for the whole crew. Some of the boys stayed with me five years. The only reason I lost some was too many young girls. But I let them take their wives on some trips upriver.

Right at the mouth of the Yukon a bar comes across the river channel and if the tide is low you can't even go out with a three foot boat. You have to drop anchor and wait for the tide. At night, just sit there with lanterns. When it came up to three and a half feet it was, "Let's go!"

We had a man down there who marked the channel. He put poles with red boards along the channel. Poles with red boards on your left side coming in and on your right going out. Later on when we had searchlights we put on four inch wide scotchlight tape so we could pick them up at night, red tape on the right side going in and white for turn stakes. There were little

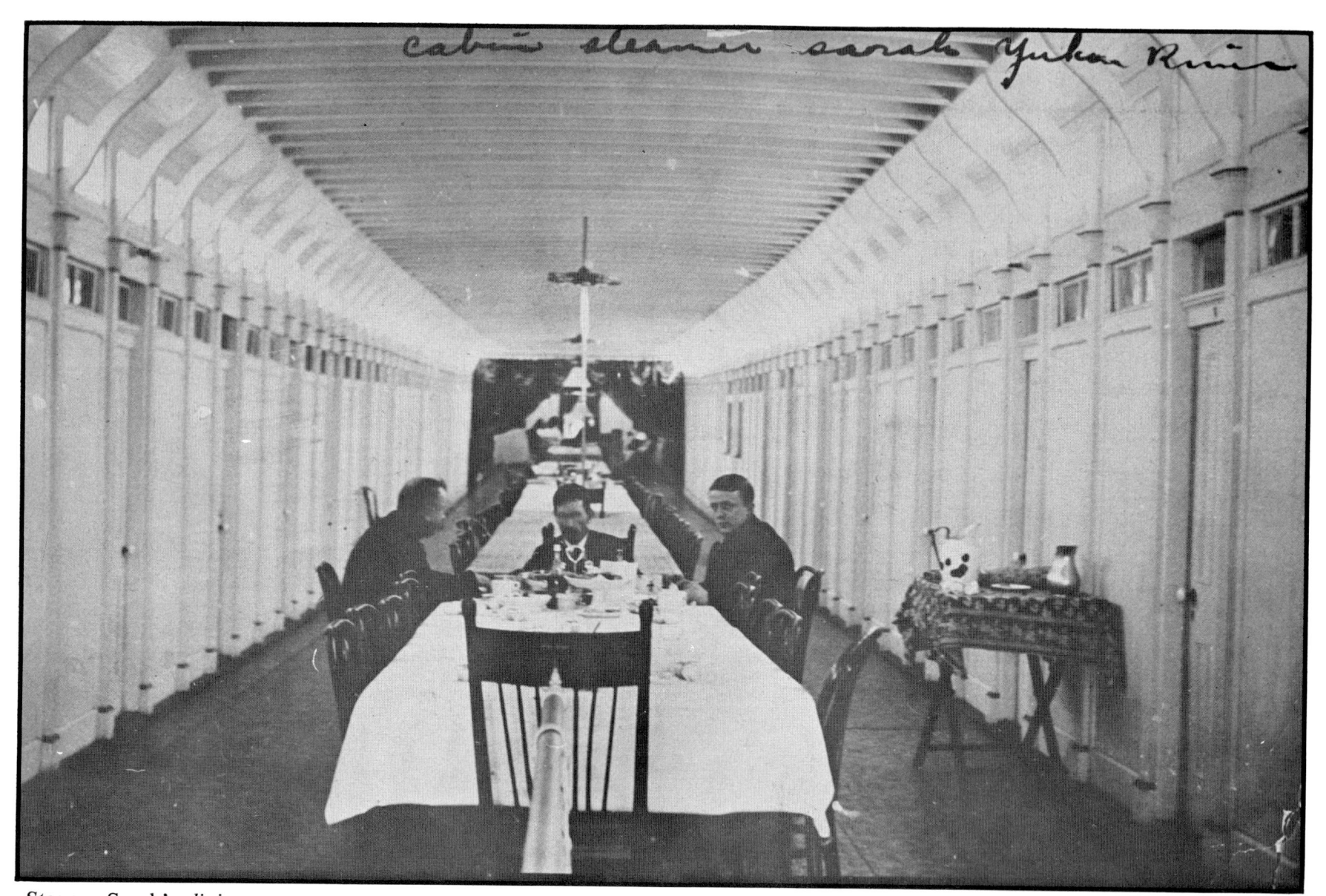

Steamer Sarah's *dining room.*

Garret Busch Collection, University of Alaska Archives

bends and one place a really bad one. You had a zigzag tight turn. The real shallow water was only 300 feet distance. Just a little hump. We'd come in until we had no more water, wait for the tide and run right over. Now they don't have anybody marking the channel and the boats are stuck there for days trying to get off.

I helped Harold Steward there lots of times. He had a big barge with a draw of four and a half feet. He was my boss but we got along. We were in steady radio communication. There was no spite like happens with some people working together.

I was one of those little muskrats, just like my father-in-law, Alex Kozevnikoff, all over the country with the boat looking for the right channel. Always looking for the best way with the least sand bars.

Mostly the Tanana River is bad for bars. Usually if we hit a bar, the barge got hung up and the boat still had enough water to float. I'd unhook the barge, twist around and get a tow line to one side of it, drop the anchor up in front of the boat and wash the bar until the barge came off. With the winch on the barge, I'd wash a little, then winch up the slack. Winch and wash, winch and wash. Pretty soon we slide right off the bar. Then I'd get into deep water, spin around to the back of the barge again and hook up.

One time we got caught around Tolovana and the Steamer *Yukon* came along. I blew the whistle and the *Yukon* turned around and helped us like we had 100 feet of water.

In 1968, NC Co. sold out their boats. I thought I was finished, but they put me on the beach. I worked in Emmonak as a timekeeper at the saltery where they salt king salmon both mild cure and hard cure. I worked there summers until 1976.

I met my wife while I was firing on the steamers. June 1928 in Marshall. We got married that November. I used to get passes for her to go home once a year to visit her folks in Hamilton. She'd go down on one trip, miss two trips and come back on the next one. Take about four weeks in all. We lived in Tanana so I'd see her during the summer each time we finished a run. But just briefly. Altogether we had three kids but we lost two when they were really young. Anna is the only one we have left. She married George Madros and they've got ten kids. I've got eleven great-grandkids too. Eleven, that's why my hair is turning grey.

Front Street in Tanana, 1904. Later, Edgar worked as a storekeeper for Northern Commercial Company. R.K. Woods Collection, University of Alaska Archives

Chapter Three: Winter Work with Dogs

Mail Carrier

I used to run dogs all over. Wintertime, nighttime, all the time. The dogs are your seeing eye anyhow. Nighttime they can see more than you can. Not only see, but they hear and smell too. We don't know exactly half of what a dog knows. His nose tells him a lot of things. And his ears are so much keener than ours.

I've been all over the spectrum. I've carried mail. I worked for the NC Company carrying mail between Tanana and Ruby. It was fun. But it was work alright. At that time we got five dollars a day and board which was good money. Other people got two and a half a day. Of course, we had long hours but gee whiz, it was alright. Didn't cost us anything to live. All we had to do, just buy some of our clothes. Dogs, sled, everything else was furnished by NC. I was too poor to have any of that.

1924 I started working for NC as an extra driver in 1924, started carrying the auditor around with dogs.

The first time I carried mail 1926. We had 800 pound load of mail for Ruby and beyond. We had two sleds. Seventeen dogs. A lot of people think, well them dogs, they don't listen. But the teams know where they're going. They know what they're going to do. That's all. No trouble.

There were horses back then too. Taking mail back and forth between Nenana and Fairbanks, Nenana and Tanana. Just in the wintertime unless it was too cold. You see in the

A ton of mail going out of Tanana across the portage. Seven or eight teams with a dozen dogs apiece. Edgar Kallands Collection.

summertime boats carry the mail. Just in the wintertime the NC Company used horse teams. They had four horse teams so one team was resting and other teams were on the trail. There was a good trail, traveled all the time.

When I was growing up it was single horses at first. Then they started using a double team with bobsled. They'd carry 1200 pounds from Nenana towards Tanana. Sometimes dogs carried mail and in '32, the airplanes started to take over.

In 1934, '35, I carried mail from Hot Springs to Tanana. Hot Springs is where they call Manley Hot Springs now. I had my own dogs then. Seven dogs was my limit. I don't know why I couldn't keep eight. One way or another I always lose a dog.

Manley Hot Springs in the 20's. The roadhouse is in the back in the middle.   *Edgar Kallands Collection*

Charlie Shade had the contract. He paid me fifty dollars a trip. I was living in Tanana at the time so fifty miles up and fifty miles back. Worked out to fifty cents a mile. No room and board and I had to provide my own dog feed. Charlie carried the mail from Nenana to Hot Springs and I'd meet him there. Carry it back to Tanana.

Hot Springs at that time was a regular mining town. There was quite a few people there. They had the roadhouse there and the NC Company. There was a good horse team trail going over the hill all the way across to another roadhouse six miles below. That was Woodchopper, a mining town one time. It was kind of dying out with maybe four or five people there.

Serum Run

I guess you know about the Iditarod Dog Race being started on account of the Serum run. I don't know why 'cause it doesn't even follow the real serum trail. Mr. Redington, Sr., he's the one that started it. Nobody said it would take but it sure has. We see all the racers going through here at Kaltag. Last winter they were everywhere in town here. They stop all over you know.

ABC from the "Wide World of Sports" was here too. They interviewed me here and in Anchorage. They took movies too. I guess on account of the Serum Run. To find out more about it. During the original run there was only two people got notoriety out of it, right in the beginning. That was Leonard Seppala and Gunner Kasten. I guess because they were the last two teams on the run. The rest of us they didn't know anything about. It was a relay so the rest of the sixteen teams didn't make it to Nome.

There were eighteen teams all together. Mr. Bob Bartlett put it in the *Congressional Record*. Only one team they left out. Said they didn't know who it was. That's the team that I gave the serum to, Dan Green. I gave it to him in Hot Springs.

If you don't know about the Serum Run there's a book written on it by Ungermann. You see, it was a diptheria epidemic in Nome. They needed serum. There was no way to get it in there outside of dog team because it was too cold. Fifty and sixty below. Horse teams was tied up on account of the weather. Airplanes couldn't fly. They was all open cockpit. So they organized the dog teams.

Governor Bone got things rolling here in Alaska. The NC Company was one of the biggest instigators of the bunch because they had mail contracts and mail teams, all the way from Nenana to Ruby.

"It was nothing when the tourists came to take in five or six hundred dollars in a couple of hours." Tanana Station. Wilson F. Erskine Collection, University of Alaska Archives

I happened to be working for the NC as an extra driver. I'd been hauling the auditor around from Tanana to Hot Springs, up to Nenana, all the way over to Circle, Fort Yukon, then retraced to Tanana. I didn't know anything about this Serum Run. I was just playing around.

I was in Tanana on account of the cold weather. John Palm in charge of the dog team and horse team mail for NC Company, said to me, "I want you to hook your dogs up tomorrow morning and make the horse team runs between here and Nenana." The next morning I was at the post office before eight. Tied my dogs. Load my sled up. Took off.

I travel twenty-five miles a day. I got into Hot Springs, went up river to Tolovana and was at Minto Roadhouse. At that time it was thirty-two more miles to Nenana. I figured, well, tomorrow I'll be in the big city. Tomorrow never came.

About five o'clock in the evening, I was laying down in the bunk, just got through feeding the dogs. The telephone rang in the roadhouse. Johnny Campbell answers, says, "Ed, that's for you."

It was T.A. Parsons, NC Agent at Nenana. He says, "I want you to go back to Tolovana."

I said, "Gee, I just left there. I'll be tomorrow in Nenana. I don't want to go back tonight. It's after five." I didn't know anything about what's going on.

"Well," he said, "there's a diptheria epidemic in Nome. The train will be in here with the serum about five o'clock tonight. They're running a special non-stop train from Seward to Nenana. We'll have relay teams running the serum to Nome. Bill Shannon is going to leave here as soon as the train gets in. I want you to meet him in Tolovanna."

Tolovana roadhouse in the spring 1915. Double ender, horsedrawn sleds for carrying passengers. Vachon Sister Mary Louise Collection, University of Alaska Archives

"What'll I do with the mail?"

He says, "Put the mail in the roadhouse."

"Fine." So I went and had something to eat. Then I hooked up the dogs and headed back. Pretty near sixty below. Beautiful moonlight night. I got to Tolovana about ten thirty or eleven o'clock. Harry Martin and another man was there. They helped me unhook the dogs, put them away, and fed them. I went in and Mrs. Martin had supper ready again for me. I watered dogs and went to bed.

Shannon came in next day about eleven o'clock. I took the serum and headed for Hot Springs. I got there about four o'clock in the afternoon. They warmed the serum up a little bit. Dan Green hooked up his dogs and took off for Fish Lake.

I had something to eat and took care of my dogs. He hadn't gotten to Fish Lake when I went to bed. That was twenty-five miles. But when I got up next morning, why, the serum was already on it's way to Ruby from Tanana.

I just took my time, hooked up and headed back to Tanana. Then we all listened to where the serum was by telephone. It was the old abandoned Army telegraph line that people took care of between Tanana and Ruby. It took five days from Nenana to Nome traveling night and day. That's over six hundred miles and more than that by dog team. They were really moving.

Between Nenana and Tanana is 132 miles. From Ruby to

Unloading freight into the new gold mining supply center named Ruby. 1912.
Alaska Historical Library

The school is the biggest building in Kaltag.

Kaltag is little over 120. It's 80 to 90 miles across the portage from Kaltag to Unalakleet. But those teams picked up momentum as they were going along. They all think, well, I'm going to beat the other fellow's time. They had lighter sleds and made good time.

We each got a citation from Governor Bone. I lost mine in the fire. And H. K. Mulford Company who developed the serum also gave us a gold medal worth twenty dollars at the time. Eighteen of us. I misplaced that one. I took it out of my pocketbook, said, "Well, I'm going to leave it home from now on. I'm liable to lose it." I guess I should have kept it in my pocketbook. Because I haven't seen it since.

That first run was about the second week in January, 1925. They had another run pretty near the last week in February. That second run was just bringing more serum to spread to different places along the line, 100 pounds in that one. First run had nineteen pounds.

I carried it that time between Nine Mile Point and Kokrines. I made that thirty-two mile run in three hours and a half going down. I'm scared to say how long it took coming back. You want to know when driving dogs is lots of fun? It took two full days to come back the same distance from Kokrines to Nine Mile Point. Twenty-six dogs and two men. Me and Mike Nickoli.

You see, we just had snow. They must have opened up the basket up there in the sky and just dropped it. When it quit snowing we had three and a half feet of snow where our trail was. I'd walk ahead ten minutes breaking trail. Then Mike would catch me with the dogs. I'd get off the snowshoes and he'd get ready and break trail. I'd wait for him for ten minutes and catch up. Oh, it was wonderful. Every step we made we'd go down over our knees. If those dogs got off our trail, they were lost. I'll tell you that was tough.

That's not the only time it was tough. It's been tough after that too. But I never even thought of giving up dogs. I liked them. They knew what I was going to do. They were good.

Trapping

I treat all my dogs the same. I had dog teams that wouldn't run away from me. I played with them all the time. That's one reason. I turn them loose and I play with them. And when I go away and come back and they're waiting for me, I pet them all right away. I wouldn't just pet one and go on. I pet the whole bunch. Anytime I got up amongst them, they were all right around me.

I had no necklines on my dogs, which gives them more freedom. They could lay down anyway they want to lay down when I walked away from the sled. There was none of this, straighten out, and never laying down this way or that. They curl up anyway they want to. And no, they didn't fight. It's all according to to the way you treat dogs. You treat them good and they're right back to you like that.

I trapped with those dogs I raised. Raised some good ones too. The only dog we couldn't make a leader out of was Gypsy. He was a wheel dog and wouldn't go anywhere else. And Rover, he was my leader only. Nobody else could drive him, only me. Well, my daughter, Anna, could drive him anywhere in town when she was nine or ten years old. Soon as she went down the bank he'd turn around and want to come back. He wouldn't take her out of the village. Period. I could drive him anywhere.

Rover was one of my six leaders out of seven dog teams. He was the last dog I ever put in lead. Somewhere in the '50's. I never had no other leader that I wanted. I walk away from the sled, that was it. Nobody could move him. And if he didn't move to go, the other dogs wouldn't go. I could walk away from the sleigh and when I come back two hours later the whole team was still there. All glad to see me.

That was when I was trapping between here and Old Woman, about forty miles from here. I didn't trap the full distance because there was people trapping from town here to about twenty miles out. I trapped from Twenty Mile on out. Two of us. Elia Stanley and I. Missouri Stanley's older brother. Trapped for mink mostly. There was no marten then. Maybe one in ten miles.

My family was in town here at that time. Anna had to go to school. I'd go out three, four, five days. Sometimes a week. Once I was out pretty near two weeks but I had plenty of wood home.

There was hardly anything out there. I was lucky to get five or six mink before Christmas. But after our daughter married George Madros we trapped beaver together out there. We did well on beaver. I took him under my wing, and kind of showed him how to set traps. I made sure the trap was set okay. When we got through that first year, we both had forty beaver each. We hadn't broken any rules because we each had two limits. I had twenty for myself and twenty for my wife. We both took our wives out to spend the night out there. We had our tent on top of three logs high, fixed up real nice and warm. It was fun.

That winter we had to trade beaver skins for fish. I was too busy working on the boats in the summer to fish for dog feed. Right there I says, "George, I'll make a deal. You fish for the dog teams and I'll make sure we've got flour, sugar, milk and the rest of our food." That's the way it's been all the way through.

When we got beaver meat we'd feed them beaver meat with fish. Believe me, that beaver meat makes them feel good too. You bet. And you can call dogs dumb if you want to, but I know different. We give them each fish and a half a day while we was trapping. They'd eat it. Then if we was going to feed them beaver meat, we'd give them only one fish. You know, them rascals wouldn't eat their fish. No. They'd sit there and wait. So George and I we went in tent and let them wait. They still waited. So we went back out and fed them the beaver meat. They ate that first.

After that first year we averaged around thirty-five beaver every year and we didn't try to kill our country. We caught beaver right up to about five years ago. Then George went to Anchorage one winter. He came back the next year. In the meantime, a couple of men went out there and just cleaned it out. Young babies and all. Killed all the houses. It's beginning to build up again now. That land belongs to Anna and George now. Nobody can trap there but them. They have a tent frame there.

I enjoyed trapping beaver more than anything else. It's harder work and all that, but I liked it. You've only got one place to set your traps and you're right there. And you're outdoors and your own boss. Period. In town, why, you really got nothing to do. Out there you've got something to do every day. We had our radio with us. Listen to the news, nighttime. We enjoyed it.

After trapping we'd go up to Koyukuk and sell most of furs to Dominic. Spend three or four days up there with him and had a good time. Marten wasn't much back then. Maybe eight or nine dollars. Big beaver blankets was running about thirty dollars.

I gave up trapping bout '58. I had a bum knee and couldn't walk on it very good. I didn't want to throw all the work on my partner. It's got to be fifty-fifty in the work when I'm out trapping. So I just quit.

Then I had surgery on my knee and that was the end of having dogs. You had to be able to walk with dogs. Because if there's lots of new snow, you have to put on snowshoes and walk ahead of the dogs for long hours. When you get on snowshoes it means lots of work. I got my first sno-go in 1961 and that was the end of it. It was the first Ski-Doo in Kaltag. I got it mostly to haul wood.

Dogs, fish racks, and boats on the beach in front of Kaltag.

Chapter Four: Kaltag Today

This chapter is largely comprised of Edgar's thoughts. It also includes some comments by his wife Virginia during the final reading of the manuscript for approval in Anchorage, March, 1981.

Store and Post Office

Virginia, the day she met the Pope in Anchorage.

I moved to Kaltag in 1935. I had a job as storekeeper for Sommers and Russell's that was going to last all winter. It was going to be one winter but it has been lots of winters. Things were easier here than in Tanana. Wood was easy to get and I could trap closer to town. In Tanana I'd have to go forty miles to find open country. More space around here. Not so many people.

I didn't listen to my wife. I should have. I'd be retired and better off now. But, no, I had to go and start this store in 1952. At first it was alright. We sold general groceries and hardware. The people brought in their furs and we did alright. For three thousand dollars plus shipping we could get all our supplies in here and last fine till March. Now prices what they are we can't get much stock for the shelves and it is gone in a few days. And people don't bring in what furs they catch. It all goes to Galena or Outside. They don't save their money to buy grub to trap out of town. It's altogether different now than it used to be.

When I first started the store we had boats coming in here

Edgar writing out a receipt in his Kaltag store.

every week. Seattle to here took two and a half or three weeks. Now it takes that long from Fairbanks. It all goes by airplane too. Anchorage to here is eighty-five minutes flying time. We got faster service while it's moving alright, but it must stop and take a rest, maybe make tea, somewhere along the line.

Far as trapping goes it is a hard way to make a living, but it can be done and a guy can have a good life from it. Now if you wanted to live high, wide, and handsome then maybe you couldn't catch enough fur. But if you just want to get your groceries, flour, sugar and lard, and fish in the summer you can have a good life.

1932-33 I got the contract to cut steamboat wood in Tanana. I bid $6.20 a cord. I put all my money into groceries and went down across the river from Kallands. My brother-in-law and Art Ambrose and I put up three or four log high walls and pitched two tents on top of them. We lived in those tents all winter and cut wood. It sure was nice living in a tent all winter out in the fresh air everyday. We didn't mind the cold because we had fire going all the time. Art, my wife Virginia, our daughter Anna and me. We lived right there and had a good time. Adam Minook, Michael Albert and I got a bear and a moose so we were set for the winter. All of us enjoyed it a lot. My wife often talks about it yet. She'd like to put in one more winter like that. The post office and store ties us both down, but when we retire, maybe then.

September 1979, fish racks on the beach in front of Kaltag.

Mother's got twenty-eight years in with the post office now. She took it over from Johnny Sommers, Sr. The pay was once every three months and amounted to about sixty dollars so he wanted to get rid of it. He showed her how to do the books and she started out like that.

We both worked for the weather bureau about then too. The year before World War II. She called in the weather to the Signal Corps from Kaltag and I did from Nulato. When they closed down Nulato I came back down here and we had around-the-clock reporting. It seems like I had to work away from home a lot to get my livelihood. Gone all summer and a lot of the winter. Not enough fur to trap that time and beaver was closed.

Father Baud got me started showing movies here. He got them into Nulato and then sent them on to me. I had the light plant operating and room in the store so it worked out pretty good. Most of them come from Pictures, Inc., but now we'll start up with Images. Some of them we make money on, some we lose.

One of my grandaughters is working in the store with me. She has to use the adding machine all the time to figure things out. I used to do that. I used an adding machine a lot working for NC Co. But I found out that if you depend on the machine all the time to figure things out you get so you can't do it with a pencil. Now all the kids use calculators in school for their math work. One or two of my grandchildren help in the store when I'm not around, but I don't like them there all the time. They help a little. Today one split wood for me and another one worked in the store a little bit. They're alright. They help a little.

When I was supplying power to the village I had two generators, a 12kw and a 5kw. AVEC came in here and bought me out. They wanted the 12kw but said the 5kw was no good. It's twenty-three years old and I've had a few problems with it but it has years of work left in it. AVEC promised cheap electricity, but it just costs me more. When I have my own plant running I have lights all over the place and it only costs half as much as when I have AVEC power with just one or two lights on. Last month my bill was $320. That's pretty high. Some of it is because I've got a hot water heater and two freezers running.

School Board

I'm on the local school board and we're supposed to help the teachers all kinds of ways with the students. Then we have to watch the teachers to see they're doing right. Whatever they're doing wrong we're supposed to correct them. We had some problem with teachers in Kaltag a couple years ago, but the school board split up on it. There were petitions going both ways on that one. I stuck up for the students who were being mistreated by the teachers. No official action was taken but all the teachers in question have left here. We've got a new principal now too. And I'm right behind him. He doesn't let the kids get away with anything. At recess there's a teacher at every door. No crowding or running anymore. And he tightened up on using the gym. If I had my way they'd close it up and not let kids in there at all after school. The only way to control the kids is to not let them in. Keep them out.

Edgar Kallands, 1981.

Summertime kids can do whatever they want outside. Year before last one of the students kept the baseball and they were out on the field practicing every night. They went to Galena for the tournament and came home with trophies. They took every game just like eating pie. This last year they gave the baseball to a school board member to take care of and paid him. Nobody practiced. I don't think they even had a tournament.

Changes

Since I've been in Kaltag it has gone downhill. It seems like now we don't have money like we used to have. The second year I was here they had a meeting about the dance hall. They had just built a new dance hall but they didn't have any roofing. They wanted to collect money for the roofing and the chief, Old Man Alexie asked me to take care of it. I got a book and wrote each man's contribution down. And this was all trapping money, you have to remember. They collected $250 that night. Next spring we had the roofing come in on the first boat.

A problem in Kaltag we talk (Edgar and Virginia) about a lot is drinking among the kids, children, teenagers, even old ladies. There's just a few families don't drink. We wish that liquor never came to town.

People work hard, get their checks and then go to Galena and charter liquor back to Kaltag. Drink up their checks. Most all of the money goes out of town. They tried to open a liquor store but people signed against it.

"I took lots of pictures while I was traveling up and down the river."

Long ago we had a liquor store in Kaltag. They'd just drink one night. And they didn't have to drink to have a dance. Not like now. I really don't know what would happen if they quit drinking. But you can't tell people what to do, they have to choose for themselves.

Everything has changed from our day. Everyone used to go out trapping, did a lot of sewing, boots and parkas. We didn't wear jackets like now. The woman did sewing. All winter long.

Now teaching school is about the only job in Kaltag, or clerk. And a few dependable people in town can haul firewood and sell it at ten dollars a sno-go load. Now people need to go to college so they can get jobs, make a living. These three last grandaughters all want to go to college. They should. But we just let them choose their way of life and hope they're happy. I don't know what kind of life they'll have in the future.

Kaltag landing. Propane bottles stacked to go out on the next barge.

Edgar Joseph and Johnny Folger on the Tanana River. They have a poling boat to go up river but they put an inboard gas engine in theirs.
Edgar Kallands Collection

Index

Alexie, Old Man 59
Able, Cris 20
Adams, George 30, 31, 35
airplane 42, 44
Alaska 14, 26, 32
Alaska Commercial 35
Albert, Michael 56
Alice 14
Ambrose, Art 56
Anchorage 43
Anicich, Joe 20
Anicich, Marie 20
army 18, 20
Barry K 32, 35
Bartlett, Bob 43
Beaver 32
beaver 51, 52
beadwork 34
boats 21, 32, 34, 42, 54
Bone, Governor 44, 48
Brooks Trail 21
Cambell, Arthur J. 20
camp 21, 32, 51, 56
Campbell, Johnny 45
cannery work 39
changes 59, 60
Chemawa 23
Chiniliak 36
Circle 32
cold 41
Dall River 21
Dawson 14, 32

death 18, 21, 26
Delta 14
disease 44
dogs 14, 15, 41-53
Dorn, Fred 35
Dow, Leon M. 28, 30
Eagle 32
economics 13, 20, 32-35, 51-57, 59, 60
education 13, 15-19, 21, 30, 31, 35, 60
electricity 58
Emmonak 39
Episcopal Mission 18
Fairbanks 14, 21, 41, 55
family 51
fishing 12, 39
food 55, 56
Fort Gibbon 16, 18
Fort Yukon 32
Galena 31, 54, 59
games 25, 37, 59
gardens 13, 19, 20
General J. W. Jacobs 14, 26
goldmining 12, 43
grandchildren 57
Green, Dan 44, 47
Green, George 14
Green, Jack 14
Hamilton 40
Harper, Jesse (Mozee) 16
healthcare 21, 31, 43-49

Holy Cross 20, 23
horses 20-23, 42, 44
Hot Springs 32, 33, 42-45, 47
houses (shelter) 13
hunting 24-26, 56
Iditarod Race 11, 43-49
Jeff Davis 14
Jetté 19
Johnson, Axel 28
Johnson, Walter 30
Julia B 14, 31
Kallands 12-15
Kallands, Alexander (father) 12, 14, 18-23
Kallands, Angeline Titi 12, 18, 21
Kallands, Anna (Madros) 40, 50
Kallands, Virginia 11, 51, 54, 56, 57
Kaltag 11, 18, 43, 48, 54, 57, 59
Kaska 14
Kasten, Gunner 43
Kee's 25
Kee, Anna Pickett 18
Kokrine, Margaret (Peterson) 18
Kokrines 15, 49
Kotlik 36
Koyukon (language) 18, 23
Langford, Mr. & Mrs. 13
language (also see Koyukon) 18
Lee's 25
liquor 22, 24, 59, 60
Little Henry 13, 15

Little Paul 13
Lockwood 25
Madros, Anna (Kallands) 40, 52, 56
Madros, George 40, 51, 52
mail 12, 41-49
Manley Hot Springs (see Hot Springs) 32, 33, 42
marriage 40
Mason Creek Slough 12
Marshall 30, 35, 40
Martin, Harry 46
Mildred 36
Minto 45
Minneapolis 14
Minook, John 13
Minook, Adam 56
missionary 13, 18, 23
mooseskin 34
Mozee, Ben 16
muskrat 25, 26
names 13
Natives 18, 23
N.C. Company 20, 35, 39, 41-45, 57,
Nenana 28, 32, 41-45, 47
Newfoundland 12
Nickoli, Mike 49
Nome 11, 12, 15, 45
Northern Navigation Company 35
Nulato 18, 57
Old Woman 50

Parsons, T. A. 45
photography 19
prohibition 22
Racey, Fred 26
Rampart 32
ratting (see muskrat)
Redington, Joe Sr. 43
Reliance 14
roadhouses 12-14, 43, 46
Roberts, Essau 23, 25
Ruby 41, 44, 47
Russell, Opie 21, 22
Sarah 14, 34, 38
school (also, education) 15-19, 58, 59
Schwatka 29
Seattle 55
Seppala, Leonard 43
serum run 43-49
Seward 32, 45
sewing 34
Shade, Charlie 43
Shannon, Bill 45, 47
shelter (see houses)
Signal Corps 57
Skagway 32
sleds 15, 48
sno-go (snowmachine) 53
snow 49
Sommers, Johnny Sr. 57
spring 26
Stanley, Elia 51

Stanley, Missouri 51
steamboats 13, 14, 16, 25-40, 56
Steven, Benjamin 25
Stevens, Belle 23
Stevens Village 17, 21, 23
Stewart, Harold 35, 39
stores 34, 35, 52, 54
St. Michael 14, 36
Susie-Louise 14, 29
Tanana River 39
Tanana 14
Tanana 12, 14-24, 31, 32, 40-47
Tolovana 39, 45, 46
tourists 32-34
trails 14, 21, 49
train 45
transportation 20, 21, 32, 43-49
trapping 50-55
Trinity Bay 12
Whitehorse 14, 26, 27
Whites 18, 32
William Isem 14
wood 13, 21, 32, 53, 56, 60
Woodchopper 43
working for wages 26, 28-53, 56, 60
young people 23, 24, 32
Yukon 14, 26, 29, 32, 35, 39
Yukon mouth 36-39
Yukon River 12, 14